Jean Stevens

Beyond Satnav

MARSDEN
THE POETRY VILLAGE
PLEASE RETURN FOR
OTHERS TO ENJOY

Indigo Dreams Publishing

First Edition: Beyond Satnav
First published in Great Britain in 2016 by:
Indigo Dreams Publishing Ltd
24 Forest Houses
Halwill
Beaworthy
EX21 5UU
www.indigodreams.co.uk

Jean Stevens has asserted her right under the Copyright, Designs and Patents Act 1988 to be identified as the author of this work.
©2016 Jean Stevens

ISBN 978-1-909357-98-3

British Library Cataloguing in Publication Data. A CIP record for this book can be obtained from the British Library.

Designed and typeset in Palatino Linotype by Indigo Dreams.
Cover photo 'Wintry Lane' by Gary Fitch.
©Hazel Fitch 2016 www.threepeaksgallery.co.uk

Printed and bound in Great Britain by 4edge Ltd.
www.4edge.co.uk
Papers used by Indigo Dreams are recyclable products made from wood grown in sustainable forests following the guidance of the Forest Stewardship Council.

Acknowledgements

I would like to acknowledge the following publications who have featured my work: Dream Catcher, The London Magazine, Orbis, Other Poetry, Pennine Platform, Poetry and Audience, Smoke, and Words.

CONTENTS

Beyond Satnav

Midnight in Cheddar Gorge

Rumbles disturb us
lightning zigzags.
We unzip flimsy canvas

inch outside to mayhem
overhead - a force between us
and the sky -

and stand, wordless,
in that narrow valley
where trapped thunder

ricochets one side of the gorge
to the other and back
colliding with new stampedes

of sound that roar non-stop
off the rock among
jagged flares

and rain that flattens
our hair, seeping
through to skin.

We gaze upwards
tiny figures exposed
in more than daylight.

Beach in Winter

Knuckleduster winds attack
as the sea rolls inland

with curled fists nothing can stop.
I'm no more valued than a punch ball.

I came to find something lost
but fear they will gang up to corrugate

my flesh, reach through to the skeleton,
gobble up my words. It will take

drudgery and a bone-hard will
to go on searching here.

Fogbow

When its fragile arc appeared
against the misty hills

I saw that my father stood
beneath the fogbow's curve

a shadow within deeper shadow
yet him in the tilt of his head

the dip of his shoulders
the hands of a man who worked

with spanner and wrench.
He said *I'm cold. So cold.*

I tried to reach him
I can make you warm

but only heard the words
You can't be where I am.

Then he was gone,
all the colours

of the world lost
in that rare white rainbow.

The Last of the Sun

Scissor-cut crags rise sheer
against the sky, cattle straddle
sloping fields, sheep graze

at an angle, daredevil starlings
wheel for home as the last
of the sun paints buttered light

on the windows of houses
stacked higgledy piggledy
across each climbing level

among the trees of Castleberg
where drystone walls weave
patchwork over the hills.

The sky gives in to dusk
and below I breathe the spikiness
of rosemary, hear a blackbird's lilt.

The garden's chilly now
time to go indoors
to artificial light.

Christmas Island and Cambridge

We saw a brilliant light
as if a radiant firebar had been
switched on in our heads. It grew
bright upon bright and in front
of closed eyes we saw the bones
in our hands like pink x-rays.

Our eyes glowed in sunlight
as we lounged by the Cam
then laughing piled into a punt.
With expert hands my lover steered,
crystal drops fell among willows,
and my fingers idled through water.

A mushroom cloud arose,
glass shattered, palm trees shook,
we were knocked clean off our feet.

Salmon, cucumber, strawberries
spilled from the hamper,
our glasses foamed with champagne,
while we lay in the green
orchard of Grantchester
looking up at unclouded blue.

And that was the day
when the blinded birds
fell from the sky.

All Week We've Waited

i.m. G.P.Stevens

All week we've waited on the edge
of the Moray Firth – seen tides recede
and surge, endured a blowtorch sun,

sandpaper winds, and lightning flaring
across black skies – watching,
watching, desperate to see dolphins.

Our final day, for five more hours we stand
then, as the tide churns between ebb and flood
and swirls up tiny fish that lure the salmon,

children's voices call – and, look:
tail and dorsal fins dip and rise along
the coast and in their element they come

easy riders of the waves, till more than
twenty breach the sea, bottle-nosed streaks
of white, dove grey and wetly shining black

who leap, fly, plunge, then soar again,
twisting high above the firth, clear against
the northern sky here on the slope of light.

We're tied to earth, part of a jockeying
crowd ankle deep in waves united in our need
to get nearer to this show of grace.

An hour or more the dolphins stay, then one
by one they lift through waves and air
in a last display of dark then light then dark.

Deluge

Steeled against whiplash wind,
like the old man I saw

queueing outside the foodbank
in a darkly dripping

raincoat, a staunch blackbird
waits on the limestone wall.

The rain's relentless –
unloads a waterfall

down the flattened feathers
bounces back up again

when it hits stone.
I wait for him

to make for shelter
or fly back to his nest

yet he sticks it out.
The clouds are thick with grey

but maybe the sky will lighten
and he'll unearth something.

Crown Point

Though forged by man
the singing ringing tree
leans like a weathered hawthorn
over the moorland edge
above the once known town.

To get there you must climb
a long pebbled road, hacked
through gorse and heather,
fight the misted wet, the gale
that hurls you back with every step.

At last you reach the sculpted steel,
adjust your eyes to the gleam
of interwoven pipes, hear the metal tree
bend the keen energy of the wind
into an unearthly song

that brings no comfort.
Except that the tree stands stoical
as a lone horse and will not move
whatever thunder lightning storm
or scorching sun.

The more wind, the more rain,
the more it will ring and sing.

Bluebells

An April ritual for us as kids
to ride our bikes to the bluebell woods
always thrilled when we glimpsed the vivid
blooms spread before us like a counterpane.

Each year we picked armfuls
knew we shouldn't
knew they'd be dead before we got home
yet every time we hoped.

Years later when I walked with you
in fresh discovered woods
masses of bluebells dazzled us
lit our day with lapis lazuli.

I want to walk again with you
I want to lie again with you
more than I ever did, against all sense
hoping that bluebells might live.

Cherry Blossom

My shoes were lined up on newspaper
on the kitchen floor
where my father knelt

his short-back-and-sides
black as the polish in the squat
round tin that smelled of tar.

Work had bruised his hands
yet he cradled each shoe
with fingers keen as a child's,

spat in the polish, swirled
a sturdy brush to make a thick pool
he smoothed into every crease

then with bitten-lipped focus
guided a softer brush
to conjure a shine.

I was soon out tomboying
kicking stones, climbing trees
stamping in puddles

but though I never asked
each time he coaxed
the leather back to its best.

Today
smelling the melted summer road
I stop and gaze at my shoes.

The Birdbox

I lift out an intricate nest
woven from twigs and grass

to find tiny featherless bodies
huddled among the moss

scraps of raw flesh
that scarcely cover fragile
bones and purple veins.

As I hold the never robins
and plan their burial

I remember the two begun
children who never quite were

and the year a fledgling
fell and I lay on the lawn
close to the shivering creature

offering drops of water
on my outstretched finger.

Cold Fell

Beneath this cold are red secrets.

The sky wakes over an earth ready
to stir as light creeps along
the fell and tests the dark

in crevices of stone where a wren
has left her nest to fall to dust
and field mice hide from sudden wings.

Warmth flows down icy slopes
green shoots break free
frost rolls back as the sun

gathers fire – reminder
of what's burning far below.

Flame

At least the plump head of a match
would rasp against its box

flare from blue to yellow to red
blacken and curl as it ate itself

carrying pain to my fingers

and, as its acrid smell
tainted the air,
leave me scorched.

What I have left of you
has no solidity.
I'm going to burn your photograph.

The Jesus Bird

His belly, face and throat are white
with a flash of yellow round the eyes
and, above brown wings and crown,
dark as eucalyptus after fire,

he flaunts a red cockscomb, this tiny
bird splashed with a lavish palette.
In flight his lanky legs and toes trail
like streamers behind a child's kite.

He ignores land to stride among the lilies
of the fluent river and, in the hunt
for food, bobs his head and flicks his tail,
rhythmic as a metronome.

On the South Alligator River
the scarlet-crested Jacana bird
walks on the water.

The Secret Motorbike

Before they crashed
on the edge of Stadil Fjord
a Lancaster Bomber's homebound crew
swerved their burning plane away
from sleeping villagers and so
saved many lives but not their own.
Eight bodies still lie caught
in quicksand inside the fuselage.

Before he volunteered
aged seventeen my cousin Bert
rocketed round an English town
revving his secret motorbike
but I only heard of his glorious escapades
long after he flew in flames across
that Danish village to a dark destination
in the heart of machinery he loved.

Fiction

She told me
she held her husband's hand
and he said *Let me go*
as he slid into another world.

Ad nauseam I've seen it on TV:
        the time left for goodbyes
        the slipping away
        the body looking warm
        and kissable.

I woke middle of the night
to ugly tearing snores
choked attempts to breathe
a rattle that still hangs
over our bed.

At once he was a blue weight
colder than Siberia.

Elephants in Zimbabwe

Troubled times. I'm the sole one
on safari. The elephants run wild

won't always come, but one parades
today, lifts his trunk in greeting,

flaps huge ears to cool me, as I climb
till high enough to scramble on.

It's solid on an elephant's back
close to deep-wrinkled, leathery

bulk sashaying through the bush
while I adjust the grip

of puny legs that ache already
trying to match his sway.

I can hardly breathe, yet smile
even when he curls his trunk around

a tree, uproots it in a second
rotates it to his mouth

demolishes the lot, and strides on
planting his feet.

I carry nothing. Have left behind
my passport, camera, bag and keys

and now all signs of the camp are gone
no buildings, no landmarks, no paths

nothing to tell where we are
and no-one but the mahout.

The sun pesters my skin
and thin air parches my throat

then we're sloshing through rivers
water inching up my shoes.

On we go through thickets of trees
smelling red earth his feet disturb

as we sway to the rhythmic swish of hide
through stiffened green and yellow grass

elephant-high and closing us in
drawing us deeper and deeper.

Held by this stoical beast
I'm taken far into forgetting

forgetting poachers and poisoners
a country at war with itself

threading back through time's needle
towards the hidden spirit here

until it's only splash, thud, sway
endless sky, bush and dust.

Stony Ford Falls

This grass along the river bank,
cropped all summer by sheep
now flattened under clamouring
boots and churned to mud,
still persists, raising green blades
among slabs of rock.

Hawthorn and rowan, lacking soil,
year after year weave their roots
through cracks within the crag
and lean thin branches over the falls
their leaves raining red, cinnamon,
copper in the autumn light.

Here, after a vicious journey,
salmon launch their dappled
silver out of a whirlpool
to jump sheer limestone
the height of a dangling man,
and fail and fall and try again

to swim through air, fly up more
cascades, then scale a horseshoe
curtain of driven water
to reach the slippery rocks
where three currents race
and fight to fling them back.

Day and night they persevere –
fish, water, grass and trees.

Beyond Satnav

A three a.m. awakening:
light from neither sun
nor moon drew us to the windows

of the isolated barn
miles from electricity
beyond satnav and phone.

Gone were paths, walls, gates
under fleeces of snow
flouncing on all sides.

We dressed without words
opened the door
of a different world

walked into a white silence
deeper than the absence
of sound, the only movement

soft flakes falling
like blossom among trees
dressed for a wedding.

We came to a stone bridge
and with blue fingers scooped
cold handfuls and along curved

parapets shaped them into men,
emptied our pockets of coins for eyes
then stood, still as the forms

we had made, until we too
seemed fragile as snow
our breath scribbled on the air.

Yew Trees

I'm tired of walking this road
hemmed in by yews
but maybe I've found a way out.

I trudge a new course.
Cold and wet, the ground's
uneven, the stones on edge,

brambles and nettles wreathed
in rain catch my clothes,
prick through to flesh,

and now there's no path.

I try to turn back but weeping
blackthorns have closed in
and daylight has gone.

Stupid to think
there'd be a shortcut.

Woodplumpton Moor

Clumps of resilient grass
the chattering wind, the trusted stranger
an underground passage to somewhere else
a place to scatter what's left.

I walk back down the hill
carrying her dust on heather I picked
remember her greaseproof packages
of cheese and oven bottom cake

and, as the years collide,
hear him when he sang for her.

Visiting Poet

That word-packed weekend you walked
into and out of our lives.

You read in the dusk-filled room
where light from the one lamp skewered
your face and scrawled a deep map of your life.

As the log fire crackled to dust
you thumbed the pages of your days
and ghosts crowded the black centres

of your eyes. Your low voice
pricked us with sharp honesty,
and our bodies and breath were stilled.

Afterwards like mist the silence rolled in
until we heard the ticking heartbeat.

But you were never afraid of the clock
and the prints you left were not in snow
but in weathered stone.

Over the years I lost my way
failed to honour your gift

so weigh me down with syllables
and take me back to midnight
to darkness, hunger and the fox.

Life and Soul

The joker's here again, lurking –
he's a scream, a regular life and soul
in a purple and green bow-tie
with a ridiculous mechanical twirl.

He fingers a dominant moustache
above a wide and redly looming smile;
there's only trickery behind
the black stare of his aviator shades.

He'll mesmerise you with his party tricks,
hocus pocus coins from behind your ear,
pull forth a string of your tawdry scarves, whisk

you to kiss-me-quick Blackpool, get you to ride
time and again on the Merry-go-round, then lure
you onto the Ghost Train and padlock you inside.

The Other Side

Australia is anchored in the sea
by shoreline cities rising in towers
of light, and strung across the outback
in between is a high wire sensed only
by the dreamer ready to walk the world.
Climb up above the vast Red Centre,
reach out to Kakadu, Jindabyne,
Oodnadatta, and Arnhem Land.

Move through searing skies, wrung-out
fiery air, to the mysterious other
side where bleached bones, vermilion earth,
ancient painted rock, and daunting empty
spaces dare you to perform an arabesque
balanced on the slender thread of poetry.

Sparrowhawk

Sinewed yellow claws
    grip the splintered arm of wood
      on the rotting garden bench.

She spreads each wing
      to show a matador's cloak
      of russet, sand and cream

as the fierce beak grasps
  every barb in turn
    to be rhythmically preened.

She breathes a birthright sun
      down to the bone;

subdues the mown grass,
    the cultivated roses,
      those invaders of her kingdom.

Every strand of every feather's
      groomed by hunger

ready for the rapid flight
  through hawthorn, holly, gorse,
    the sudden snatch and kill.

Red Light

I strayed from the known route
into a dark street,
a different world of scary
shadows and black corners.
Already off balance, I stumbled

into the glaring light thrown
from a thrusting bay window.
There on display a woman
looked out on the city,
her perfect curves visible

under whispers of chiffon.
Even in that cruel light
she glowed – unbelievably beautiful.
Her eyes flashed me a message
and, though foreign to each other,

a shared language passed
between us – that knowingness
vis-à-vis men. But her smile
shook me as thread by thread
her gaze unravelled my disguise.

Encased in my tourist clothes
I was the one who seemed naked.

Classic Horse

Grey Ghost, retired from the race
and grown shabby, still had that gaze
that recognises human fear and folly
and, as I fought with bridle and bit,
he put up with my lack of grace.

All week he walked on cobble and tarmac,
high-stepped loose sand and ruffled waves,
trotted with care on the beaten earth,
till I thought I was boss and leaned that day
to push open the gate of the sea-top field.

The moment his hooves touched grass
he took back his glory and carried my life
to a winged gallop as my feet jerked clear
of the stirrups and we hurtled over the turf
to the edge of the crumbling cliff.

Elated by fear, I gave up the reins,
flung my hands forward to clutch
the far reach of his mane, and laid
my head against his outstretched neck,
a slave to the instinct in his blood.

That day I survived but soon
I shall need those old audacious
hooves to transport me once more
over the fields to the waiting edge
then take that terrible leap into space.

Except

I've never been a thief
except that time
I stole a postage stamp from Woolworths
just for the word *Tanganyika*.

Oh, yes, and the time
I took a book from Waterstones to show
the man I fancied that I wasn't
a cautious wimp.

I suppose I cheated
the bus company
once or twice jumping
on and off between stops.

But when I should have known better
I really came into my own
seized your hobbies, your voice,
conned the heart out of you.

A Wedding Wish

for Alison and Tim

Do you remember a vast mysterious
landscape where White Cliffs
nestled underground among
iridescent opal; and the night
in the outback silence when nothing
stirred and the ebony sky blazed
with the light of the moon and stars.

> *Today and forever*
> *I wish you the light of the stars.*

Beneath your feet in Broken Hill
lay garnet and silver and golden
beryl where out of desert dust
wild peaches grow and sandstone
sculptures rise; and from the Line of Lode
you watched a rose and saffron sunset
paint the Silver City.

> *Today and forever*
> *I wish you the sparkle of silver.*

Walking the Dales in winter by the crags
of Pen-y-ghent you revelled in snow and ice
hung in glittering necklaces along
the drystone walls, and climbed limestone
pavements where saxifrage breaks
through rock and out of nothing
creates gold and crimson flowers.

> *Today and forever*
> *I wish you the joy of saxifrage.*

For I wish you day after day
and night after night
of stars and silver and saxifrage.

Man in a Bowler Hat
René Magritte

Cutting across the canvas
is a gateless wall of cream brick.

Outside the wall a figure stands
who, like a disaster payout man, wears
a uniform bowler hat. See-through as glass
his body forms a wine bottle, his head
and neck the crystal neck, the edge
of his hat the rim, its round top the cork.

Inside his head above imagined eyes
a pale curve of moon in a dusk-blue
sky merges with the glow of a lost sun.
A sweep of lawn within the man yet beyond
the wall draws the eye forward through
brick into the longed-for garden.

There, clusters of perfect trees
frame a child's impossible house
with sturdy chimney, door without
a lock; and, in each window,
warm yellow light – light at the point
where his heart would beat.

Whether or not he looks forward
or back, he haunts his own life.

On the Train

Voices serious
as bishops in crisis
they make urgent points:
Is the plan working?
Who can be trusted?
What needs to happen today?

I stop writing, look up.
Partisan scarves roll
into focus; one man leans
forward, his eyes a blue fire:
I don't mind us losing
if players show passion.

They journey miles to witness
hacked shins on their gods
balls bouncing off woodwork
dubious red cards –
with the likelihood
there's a dodgy ref.

Geared up for the brief
staged battle they're ready
for their hearts to stop.

I click my biro shut
look out for my station
take these words with me:

Show some passion
and don't mind losing.

Like Cauliflowers

After G.K. Chesterton

Look, she said, *It's just like cauliflowers.*
A country girl, she'd never seen the sea.

Now, the sea makes me think of cabbages
just as cabbages, with their mingled
violet and green, remind me of the sea

in which a purple nearing red may ripple
through a green that's almost yellow,
and yet remain the blue sea as a whole.

Then there's the repetition of the curves
of the cabbage curling over like waves.
But cauliflowers show that waves not only curl

but break to branching foam, bubbling
and opaque. They show the sturdy lines
of life, even as the arcs of rushing water

show all the energy of verdant stalks,
and the sea appears a limitless green
plant holding one immense white flower.

Nasturtiums at Midnight

Among zimmers and pills
and the other old, she gropes
for a language to coax
her memories from the dark:

Was there once a waterfall
of snow, nasturtiums at midnight,
that haloed eclipse of the moon?
Was there a rainbow in the breeze?

Was there the bliss of birches
donating their leaves
wings swooping from nettles
bells rising from the plains
mist wreathing the horses
where green was mown and the soil
turned and harvested?

Untitled

Blood was wasted every month
dropping away to nothing.

Nine years she yearned
until what entered her stayed

occupied body and mind
as she prepared the house.

When the pains began
husband and home were under rubble.

She gave birth among strangers
to a beautiful ticking bomb.

Long After the War

after the aerial dogfight
after the flames and the crash
after a journey of sixty-five years
after news of the other dead

my finger traced a family name
carved in foreign stone.

Back home, I find an invasion:
slimy weeds, rank grass,
thistle, nettle, dandelion
have risen and claimed the garden
blackfly, slugs and mice
have ravaged the land.
Even the roses are rotting.

All I can do
to deal with this
is reach for the petrol can.

T-shirt

Hot, hot in Top End Darwin
watching midnight films
from deckchairs
steeped in the day's sun.

Aboriginal stories
watched under unknown stars
were dreamtime to two pale Poms

and you wanted a keepsake.
The t-shirt was too small
but you loved its words:

Deckchair Theatre
yellow and red against black.

It doesn't fit me either
but I still keep it.

I'm here

I'm inside this lissom body
with the butterfly tattoo
and lots of attitude.

I'm the fat one invading
your holiday snap
shabby dress, frizzy hair.

I'm inside these polished pecs
with a six-pack underneath
my eyes on the blonde with the tits.

I'm in Rome with the other
visiting nuns putting my faith
in the Pope.

I'm behind the balaclava
dreaming where bullets
will tear into flesh.

I'm trapped in the centre
of Wellington's square
moved forward by other men's feet.

Rummage

At Heathrow he upturned
my handbag. His eyes and fingers
groped my life: the too-young

scarlet lipstick, Blake's poems
Stolen from Burnley Library,
a key for which I never found a lock.

A mobile phone – not your
smart kind – my passport with its
crushing photograph. A number –

who to contact in case of ...
My debit card. That letter opened
and folded a hundred times

a theatre ticket stub for *Lear*,
the grubby hanky used with spit
to clean bird shit off the car.

He gripped the shabby fabric
pulled the bag inside out, found
the sprigs of rosemary and rue.

Winter in Yorkshire

It's white over in the Dales.
After freezing fog comes

snow-crumb, rime frost
that turns mucky fields

to sparkling hillsides with their scars
of broken skeleton and shell

marbles the plateaus of rock -
rough limestone pavements

grit down to the bone.
These pavements born of scouring ice

are mosaics of clints and grykes
constantly carved as rain and snowmelt

seep into potholes and caves.
In narrow gaps, craggy hawthorns

are honed to living sculpture
by the chill and fettling wind

among bloody cranesbill, baneberry,
rigid buckler and limestone fern.

The Spade

In the new shed,
tidy as none before,
the spade is stuck in the corner,
soil from previous gardens
crusted on its blade.

I kneel on the path by borders
he never knew, stab the earth
with a trowel, fail in the fight
against thistles – even through my
padded gloves they draw blood.

I need the spade
to dig deep into clay,
prepare the ground for harvest,
but can't even bear the weight
of this grave-digging tool.

Ripped Canvas

Miró ripped canvas
threw bombs of paint, railed
over the death of his friend
by torture and garrotte.

He splashed scarlet
created room-sized paintings
crawling with bodies
and scattered entrails

a journey to the edge
of madness, kicking
everything on the way,
an attempt to speak.

What he painted finally
is a line that judders, curling
again and again where the wrist
made painful turns

then stops abruptly:
grief packed
into one thin black line
tight as cutting wire.

Miles

At last, the crown of the hill
a pause from the aches of climbing
past the run-down houses, the unfrocked
church turned to cool apartments
past the dandelioned tennis courts
and the manor hall no longer lit
where now a bird flashes through
the unroofed rafters.

The moor opens out like a green book
along each side of the spine I tread
doesn't seem smaller than when
I roamed here as a child or less
full of mystery than when exploration
was everyday. It's years since I left
and I'm not sure why I've come back.
I shall walk for miles counting the horizons.

This Great Beech

This great beech merges with
my life. Each day its canopy
of wind-carved branches filters

nuances of sun as if through lace
dictates where I can work
what will grow in my garden

gathers a weight of water
and waits to rain on me
when no-one else gets wet

harnesses the wind to fling
down snapped limbs and a whip
of twigs. Ring upon ring inside

the massive trunk show it has
seen at least four generations
of cradles come and coffins leave

this house. Mere feet away
it spreads persistent roots beneath
grass, terrace, kitchen,

living room and hall,
an unseen world growing
right under my feet.

Winter Light

A low sun dazzles
through trees stripped
back to tracery
dripping with rain

that reflects
yellow and red against
drystone walls and across
patterned fields.

Nothing so cosy as a rainbow
but still a procession of light
where the farmer grinds
his rusty tractor over earth
and landlocked seabirds wait.

Indigo Dreams Publishing Ltd
24, Forest Houses
Cookworthy Moor
Halwill
Beaworthy
Devon
EX21 5UU
www.indigodreams.co.uk